CROCKPOT RECIPES

50 DELICIOUS SLOW COOKER DESSERT RECIPES

From Betty's Kitchen to Yours!

©Copyright

All Rights Reserved

Betty AKA "Betty Crockpot"

A special message from Betty

Hi, I am Betty but my friends all call me Betty Crockpot. I have spent most of my life in the kitchen where I am in my comfort zone and able to do what I enjoy best. I want to share only the best crockpot and slow cooker recipes with you and your family. I only hope that you will enjoy them as much as my family does. Thanks!

Betty

Table of Contents

Introduction

1) Carrot pudding

2) Chocolate risotto

3) Coconut and Mocha Poached Pears

4) Lemon and cherry pudding

5) Chocolaty walnut pudding

6) Fig stuffed apples

7) Crispy Apricot

8) Dry fruits vermicelli pudding

9) Butter scotch fondue

10) Leftover bread and chocolate pudding

11) Caramel Pears

12) Chocolate and peanut butter cake

13) Streusel pound cake

14) Orange in apple cider

15) Apple Cranberry Compote

16) Strawberry Cobbler

17) Slow cooked cranberries

18) Slow cooked ginger bread

19) Classic bread pudding

20) Pumpkin bread

21) Fruit Compote

22) Banana and coconut slow pudding

23) Delicious Tapioca Pudding

24) Sweet potato casserole

25) Gooey chocolate cake

26) Pistachio and honey cake

27) Crockpot Chocolate fudge

28) Slow cooker cherry pound cake

29) Crockpot Candy

30) Slow cooker crème brulee

31) Crockpot mango cheesecake

32) Crockpot squash and pineapple

33) Pineapple peach fusion

34) Butterscotch cocoa

35) Banana Lemon pudding

36) Marshmallow chocolate fondue

37) Blueberry dumplings

38) Chocolate and peppermint pretzels

39) Crockpot Orange Cinnamon pudding

40) Slow cooked apples with peanut butter

41) Banana Foster

42) Tiramisu Pudding

43) Coconut and Tapioca pudding

44) Vanilla flavored pudding with Brandy

45) Dark Apple Cake

46) Gooey Chocolate brownie cake

47) Cherry sauce to go with Angel Cake

48) Slow Cooker Carrot cake

49) Pumpkin Pie dip

50) Slow cooked pear with apples

Hey check this out!

Introduction

Thank you for downloading this eBook. Who can resist the temptation of gorging on a yummy dessert, especially if it is slow cooked with a dash of love? We present you 50 such delicious crockpot dessert recipes that will keep you wanting for more. These recipes are simple and the preparation process has been further simplified using through step by step instructions.

There are cheesecake recipes, pudding recipes, moist cake recipes and even some yummy dips. The best part about cooking your food in a slow cooker is that even on a lazy Sunday afternoon you can put your feet up and relax while your food is being cooked with a lot of love in a Crockpot. The result is not only uber-delicious dishes but also some effortless cooking.

Our aim is to provide you easy recipes using simple ingredients that you can buy from a local market. And if you happen to run out of one of the ingredients mentioned in the recipe, we offer you some variations too. If you follow the exact recipes in this eBook, you are sure going to get a lot of attention from your loved ones. The dessert recipes mainly involving a lot of fruits are extremely mouth-watering.

Enjoy!

50 Crockpot Dessert Recipes

1) Carrot pudding

Ingredients

- 500 gm carrots (peeled and grated)
- 2 tablespoons ghee (clarified butter)
- 100 ml almond milk
- 75 ml double cream
- 6 tablespoons white sugar
- 9-10 almonds
- ½ teaspoon cardamom powder
- 9-10 chopped cashews
- 50 gm raisins

Preparation

1. In a slow cooker, take some ghee and sauté the grated carrots for 10-12 minutes.
2. Now add all the ingredients, cover the lid and let it cook for 2-2.5 hours.

Serving

Serve in a glass bowl and garnish with some pistachios on top.

2) Chocolate risotto

Ingredients

- 650 ml milk
- 150 gm rice
- 100 gm sugar
- 150 gm semi-sweet chocolate (melted)
- Whipped cream
- 2 drops of vanilla essence

Preparation

1. In a slow cooker, combine all the ingredients except chocolate and whipped cream. Let the mixture cook on medium heat for about 2.5 hours.

2. Once done, slowly pour the melted chocolate in the rice pudding, stir and let it sit for 1—12 minutes. Give another stir to mix well. Refrigerate it for 30-45 minute before serving.

Serving

Serve this risotto chilled and garnish with cinnamon sticks.

Variation

If you have run out of vanilla essence, you can do without it.

3) Coconut and Mocha Poached Pears

Ingredients

- 400 gm ripe pears (sliced in quarters)
- 100 gm brown sugar
- 100 ml coconut milk
- 70 gm coffee
- 1/4th teaspoon cinnamon powder
- 1 tablespoon dark chocolate powder
- Whipped cream for garnish

Preparation

1. Place the sliced pears in the slow cooker. Mix sugar, coconut milk, cinnamon, coffee and cocoa powder in a bowl. Pour the mixture over the pears.

2. Cook this mixture for 3.5-4 hours until the pears are tenderized.

Serving

Serve it with some whipped cream on top.

Variation

You can also use apples instead of pears.

4) Lemon and cherry pudding

Ingredients

- 250 gm fresh cherries (seeds removed)
- 3 eggs
- 100 gm sugar
- 2 teaspoon lemon rind
- 2 tablespoons lemon juice
- 1/4th teaspoon salt
- 100 gm black grapes
- 175 ml almond milk
- 2 ½ tablespoons butter
- 75 gm self-rising flour

Preparation

1. Beat the egg yolks until fluffy. Add oil, sugar, lemon juice, flour, milk and beat it using an electric mixer until it blends well. Now beat the egg whites until they are fluffy and fold them into this mixture.
2. Cook this pudding for 2-2.5 hours.

Serving

Serve it chilled and top it up with nuts.

Variation

You can use blueberries or strawberries for making this pudding.

5) Chocolaty walnut pudding

Ingredients

- 175 gm semi-sweet chocolate (melted)
- 150 gm cocoa powder
- 3 eggs (slightly beaten)
- 400 gm slightly crushed cinnamon bread
- 150 gm chopped walnuts
- 400 ml milk
- 50 gm powdered sugar

Preparation

1. Grease the slow cooker base with some butter. Heat the milk, add melted chocolate, sugar cocoa powder and whisk smooth.

2. Beat the eggs with the chocolate mixture, add walnuts and crushed bread to the slow cooker and cook for 2.5 hours.

Serving

Serve the pudding with some whipped cream on top.

Variation

You can also use almonds instead of walnuts.

6) Fig stuffed apples

Ingredients

- 4-5 green apples
- 125 gm dried figs (chopped)
- 75 gm sugar
- ½ teaspoon cinnamon powder
- 75 ml apple juice
- 1 tablespoons margarine

Preparation

1. Slice off the top 1/4th part of the apple and scoop out the remaining part. Take the figs, sugar and cinnamon powder in a bowl and mix well.
2. Now stuff this mixture into the apples using a narrow spoon.

3. Coat the apples with margarine and pour the apple juice on them.
4. Cook it for 4-4.5 hours.

Serving

Serve the apples with some honey on top.

Variation

You can use butter instead of margarine and raisins instead of figs.

7) Crispy Apricot

Ingredients

- 350 gm apricots
- 200 gm dry fruits
- 175 gm granola
- 125 gm slightly roasted desiccated coconut
- 2 tablespoons honey

Preparation

1. Grease the slow cooker with some oil. Place a layer of the dry fruits and apricots at the base of the slow cooker.
2. Mix the granola and desiccated coconut and sprinkle it on top of the dry fruits layer. Cook for 2.5 hours. Once done, top it up with honey.

Serving

You can serve this yummy dish with some Greek yogurt.

Variation

Use the same recipe.

8) Dry fruits vermicelli pudding

Ingredients

- 175 gm vermicelli (slightly roasted)
- 200 ml milk (reduced)
- 200 ml condensed milk
- 7-8 almonds
- ½ teaspoon cinnamon powder
- 8-9 raisins
- 200 gm sugar
- 1 teaspoon clarified butter
- 1 drop of rose essence
- 5 Saffron strands

Preparation

1. In a slow cooker, take some butter, add almonds, raisins and sauté them for 4-4 minutes.
2. Add vermicelli, milk, condensed milk, saffron strands cinnamon, sugar and cook for 2 hours. Once cooled down, add rose essence and mix well.

Serving

Always serve this pudding slightly chilled.

Variation

You can use rice instead of vermicelli.

9) Butter scotch fondue

Ingredients

- 400 ml condensed milk
- 100 gm butter
- 75 ml corn syrup
- 1 teaspoon vanilla essence
- 75 ml milk
- Assorted fruits

Preparation

1. Combine all the ingredients in a slow cooker and cover the lid.
2. Cook this fondue for about 3 hours.

Serving

Serve the fondue with strawberries, mango, pineapple, apple or any other fruit.

Variation

Use the same recipe.

10) Leftover bread and chocolate pudding

Ingredients

- 175 gm semi-sweet chocolate (melted)
- 3 eggs (beaten)
- 5-6 dates (seeds removed and chopped)
- 125 gm cocoa powder (Hershey)
- 400 gm cinnamon bread (slightly crushed)
- Whipped cream

Preparation

1. Heat the milk until it is slightly warm. Now add melted chocolate, dates, cocoa powder and mix it well.
2. Now add the bread, mix well and cook the pudding for 2.5 hours. Let it sit for another 30 minutes.

Serving

Serve the pudding with some almonds or whipped cream on top.

Variation

You can replace the dates with figs or raisins.

11) Caramel Pears

Ingredients

- 5-6 pears with stems
- 100 gm maple syrup
- 125 gm caramel sauce
- 1/4th teaspoon cinnamon
- ½ teaspoon lemon rind

Preparation

1. Grease the slow cooker with some butter. Lay the pears in the cooker.
2. Now mix the caramel sauce, maple syrup, lemon rind and cinnamon in a bowl.
3. Pour this mixture on top of the pears and cook for 2.5-3 hours.

Serving

Serve it with some ice cream and chocolate sauce.

Variation

The same recipe can be used for making caramel apples.

12) Chocolate and peanut butter cake

Ingredients

- 350 gm chocolate cake mix
- 125 ml melted chocolate
- 100 gm peanut butter
- 100 gm chopped dry fruits
- 100 ml milk

Preparation

1. Mix all the ingredients well in a bowl.
2. Pour it into the slow cooker and cook for 2.5-3 hours.

Serving

Serve it with some chocolate sauce on top.

13) Streusel pound cake

Ingredients

- 450 gm pound cake mix
- 150 gm brown sugar
- 1 tablespoon self-rising flour
- 100 gm walnuts or almonds
- ½ teaspoon cinnamon powder

Preparation

1. In a bowl combine all the ingredients and mix well.
2. Pour it into a slow cooker and cook for 3-4 hours.

Serving

Serve this cake with some more nuts on top.

14) Orange in apple cider

Ingredients

- 3 Oranges peeled or sliced
- 1 liter apple cider
- 1 teaspoon cloves
- 2 cinnamon sticks
- 50 gm powdered sugar

Preparation

1. Add apple cider to the slow cooker. Now add the remaining ingredients and stir well.
2. Cook on low heat for 7-8 hours.

Serving

Store it in the refrigerator and serve it chilled.

15) Apple Cranberry Compote

Ingredients

- 5 apples (peeled and sliced)
- 200 gm cranberries
- 175 gm brown sugar
- ½ teaspoon orange zest
- 100 ml water
- 50 gm port wine

Preparation

1. In a bowl, combine cranberries, sugar, orange zest, water and port wine.
2. Now place the sliced apples in a slow cooker. Pour the cranberry mixture on top and cook for 5-6 hours.

Serving

Add a dollop of whipped cream on top.

Variation

You can use white sugar instead of brown.

16) Strawberry Cobbler

Ingredients

- 400 gm biscuit chunks
- 125 gm brown sugar
- 1/ teaspoon cinnamon powder
- 100 gm butter
- 300 pie filling
- 200 gm chopped strawberries

Preparation

1. Place the biscuit chinks in the slow cooker. In a bowl combine sugar, cinnamon, butter and pour it over the biscuits.
2. Sprinkle the pie filling on top and cook for 2-2.15 hour.

Serving

Serve this dish with some strawberries on the side.

Variation

You can use a bit of cardamom powder instead of cinnamon.

17) Slow cooked cranberries

Ingredients

- 500 gm cranberries
- 250 gm brown sugar
- 100 ml water
- 1 tablespoon honey
- 9-10 roasted almonds

Preparation

1. Combine all the ingredients except the almonds in a slow cooker and cover the lid.
2. Cook the cranberries for 2-3 hours. Once cooled, drizzle some honey on top.

Serving

Serve the cranberries with some chopped roasted almonds on top.

Variation

You can replace the cranberries with blueberries or strawberries.

18) Slow cooked ginger bread

Ingredients

- 400 gm ginger-bread mix
- 75 gm sweet corn flour
- ½ teaspoon salt
- 250 ml milk
- 100 gm raisins

Preparation

1. Combine all the ingredients in a bowl and mix well. Ensure there are no lumps.
2. Pour the mixture into a cake mould. Place it on a metal rack.
3. Take about 300 ml water in the slow cooker. Now place the metal rack in the slow cooker and cook for 3-4 hours.

Serving

This bread can be served with a cup of tea each morning.

Variation

You can add some more minced ginger to get a strong flavor.

19) Classic bread pudding

Ingredients

- 400 gm bread cut into cubes
- 2 eggs (slightly beaten)
- 4 drops of vanilla essence
- 1/ teaspoon cardamom powder
- ¼ teaspoon salt
- 400 ml milk
- 125 gm brown sugar
- 100 gm dry fruits

Preparation

1. Combine eggs, vanilla essence, cardamom, salt, milk, sugar and dry fruits in a bowl. Now throw in the bread slices.

2. Pour the mixture into a backing mould. Place the mould on a trivet.
3. Pour 200 ml water in the slow cooker and place the trivet in it.
4. Cook for 2-2.15 hours.

<u>Serving</u>

Serve this dessert slightly chilled.

<u>Variation</u>

You can also use a bit of condensed milk for this pudding.

20) Pumpkin bread

Ingredients

- 300 gm chopped pumpkin
- 100 ml oil
- 100 gm sugar
- 2 eggs (beaten)
- 100 gm brown sugar
- 1/ teaspoon salt
- 1/4th teaspoon nutmeg
- 1 teaspoon soda
- 100 gm almonds (chopped)

Preparation

1. In a bowl add the eggs, sugar, oil, salt, nutmeg and almonds. Mix well. Now slowly add flour, soda and pumpkin. Combine it properly.

2. Pour this mixture into cake moulds and place the mould on a metal rack.
3. Fill the slow cooker with about 200 ml hot water and place the rack in it.
4. Cook for 2.5-3 hours.

Serving

This bread is best served with any type of fresh fruit juice.

Variation

You can use white sugar instead of brown.

21) Fruit Compote

Ingredients

- 300 gm chopped pineapples
- 400 gm sliced peaches
- 200 gm pears (chopped)
- 5-6 tablespoons orange juice
- 1 tablespoon corn flour
- 3-4 tablespoons powdered white sugar

Preparation

1. Combine the orange juice, sugar, corn flour and mix well.
2. Place the peaches, [pineapples, pears at the bottom of the Crockpot.

3. Pour the orange juice mixture on the fruits and cook for 2-3 hours.

Serving

Serve the fruit compote slightly chilled and garnish with nuts.

Variation

You can also use brown sugar instead of white sugar.

22) Banana and coconut slow pudding

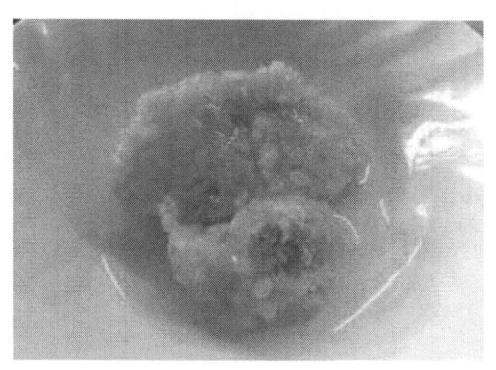

Ingredients

- 4 ripe bananas (chopped)
- 150 gm freshly shaved coconut
- 350 ml milk
- 125 gm powdered sugar
- ½ teaspoon cinnamon powder

Preparation

1. Combine all the ingredients together in a slow cooker and cover with a lid.
2. Cook the pudding for about 2-2.5 hours.

Serving

Serve this pudding with some coconut ice-cream or garnish it with banana slices.

Variation

You can also use desiccated coconut instead of a fresh one.

23) Delicious Tapioca Pudding

Ingredients

- 100 gm tapioca
- 600 ml coconut milk
- 1 teaspoon vanilla essence
- 2-3 teaspoons of orange juice
- 150 gm sugar

Preparation

1. Combine all the ingredients in a slow cooker and cover with a lid.
2. Cook for about 3.5-4 hours.

Serving

You can serve this pudding in attractive glassware.

24) Sweet potato casserole

Ingredients

- 3 sweet potatoes (softened, peeled and grated)
- ½ teaspoon vanilla essence
- ½ teaspoon cardamom powder
- 100 gm powdered sugar
- 50 gm melted butter

Preparation

1. Lay the grated sweet potatoes at the bottom of the slow cooker.
2. Combine all other ingredients in a bowl and pour the mixture on top of the sweet potatoes.
3. Cook for 3 hours.

Serving

Serve it with some caramel sauce or honey on top.

Variation

You can also use some palm or date jaggery instead of refined sugar.

25) Gooey chocolate cake

Ingredients

- 400 gm chocolate cake mix
- 225 ml water
- 3 eggs (beaten)
- 75 ml oil
- 300 ml chilled milk
- 350 gm of chocolate pudding mix
- 350 gm semi-sweet chocolate

Preparation

1. Combine cake mix with eggs, water, oil and beat it for about 2-3 minutes. Pour this mixture into a cake mould. Lay the mould on a trivet.

2. In a bowl, mix the milk and pudding mix, blend it for a minute. Pour this mixture on top of the cake mixture.
3. Cook for about 3 hours. Let it sit for another 20 minutes to cool down.

<u>Serving</u>

Chocolate cake is best served with vanilla ice-cream.

<u>Variation</u>

If you do not wish to use the cake mix, you can go the old fashioned way and make a cake mix yourself.

26) Pistachio and honey cake

Ingredients

- 150 gm melted butter
- 3-4 eggs (beaten)
- 100 gm powdered sugar
- 1 teaspoon orange zest
- 100 gm pistachios (chopped)
- 150 gm self-rising flour
- 3 ½ tablespoons honey

Preparation

1. Combine the eggs, sugar and honey in a bowl and beat them until smooth.
2. Add the flour, orange zest and pistachios.

3. Pour this mixture into a greased baking mould. Place the mould on a trivet.
4. In a slow cooker, take about 250 ml hot water. Place the trivet in the cooker and cook for 2 hours.

Serving

This cake is best served with some honey and cinnamon mixture on top.

Variation

You can also use almonds instead of pistachios.

27) Crockpot Chocolate fudge

Ingredients

- 450 gm chocolate chips
- 75 ml coconut milk
- 2-2.5 teaspoons peppermint essence
- ¼ th teaspoon salt
- 1 teaspoons melted butter

Preparation

1. Combine all the ingredients in a bowl and mix well.
2. Cover the lid and cook this mixture in the Crockpot for about 2 hours. Now cook it again for another 601 minutes without the lid.

Serving

Use a sharp knife to gently slice up this fudge and store it in the refrigerator.

Variation

You can use chocolate cubes instead of chocolate chips.

28) Slow cooker cherry pound cake

Ingredients

- 400 gm cake mix
- 150 fresh cherries (seeds removed)
- 25 ml red wine
- 3 eggs (beaten)
- 4 tablespoons flour

Preparation

1. Stir in the flour slowly into eggs and red wine. Add the cherries.
2. Gently fold in the cake mix into the cherry mixture.
3. Cook for 3.5-4 hours.

Serving

Serve in a plain white dish along with vanilla ice cream.

Variation

You can do without the red wine.

29) Crockpot Candy

Ingredients

- 450 grams roasted peanuts (unsalted)
- 350 gm chocolate chips
- 450 gm almond bark

Preparation

1. Grind the peanuts slightly in a grinder. Combine peanuts, chocolate chips, almond bark in a Crockpot.
2. Cook the mixture for about 2-2.5 hours.
3. Now scoop out a few candies out of the mixture and refrigerate them for a while.

Serving

Serve this on a large white dish.

Variation

You can add almond to this recipe too.

30) Slow cooker crème brulee

Ingredients

- 4 egg yolks (beaten)
- 5 tablespoons sugar
- 400 ml heavy cream
- ½ teaspoon vanilla essence
- 2 tablespoons castor sugar for garnish.

Preparation

1. Combine beaten eggs with sugar, cream, vanilla and give it a whisk.
2. Fill the slow cooker with about 200-250 ml water at the base.
3. Fill the cream mixture into ramekins and place them in the slow cooker. Cook them for 2 hours.

Serving

Once cooled down, sprinkle some sugar on top and use a blow torch to caramelize them.

Variation

Use the exact recipe.

31) Crockpot mango cheesecake

Ingredients

- 400 gm cream cheese
- 200 gm mango pulp
- 100 gm castor sugar
- 1 tablespoon self-rising flour
- 1/ teaspoon vanilla
- 150 gm digestive biscuit crumbs
- 2 tablespoons sugar
- 2 tablespoons butter

Preparation

1. For the base, mix the biscuit crumbs, butter and sugar in a bowl. Now spread this mixture evenly

at the base of the cake mould. Refrigerate it for 30 minutes until it becomes firm.

2. In another bowl, combine mango pulp, sugar, Flour, vanilla and pour this mixture on top of the cake base in the mould. Place the cake mould on a metal rack.

3. Fill the slow cooker with about 250 ml water. Place the rack in the cooker and cook for 2.5-3 hours.

Serving

Refrigerate this cook for about an hour after it cools down and serve it a slightly chilled.

Variation

You can use strawberry pulp instead of mango.

32) Crockpot squash and pineapple

Ingredients

- 1 butternut squash (diced)
- 500 gm chopped pineapple
- 150 gm brown sugar
- 1 teaspoon cinnamon

Preparation

1. Combine all the ingredients in a slow cooker and over the lid.
2. Cook it for 6-7 hours

Serving

Top it up with a few dry fruits or drizzle some honey on top.

33) Pineapple peach fusion

Ingredients

- 4 chopped peaches
- 350 gm chopped pineapple
- 75 ml pineapple juice
- 2 teaspoons cornstarch mixed in some pineapple juice
- 1/4th teaspoon salt
- ½ teaspoons cardamom powder
- 125 gm quinoa
- 60 gm margarine
- 2 tablespoons sugar

Preparation

1. Combine all ingredients in a bowl and mix well. Add in the cornstarch mixture too.
2. Transfer this mixture into a slow cooker and cook for about 2.5 hours.

Serving

Serve with some castor sugar on top.

Variation

You can replace the pineapple with strawberries or cranberries.

34) Butterscotch cocoa

Ingredients

- 350 gm butterscotch chocolate chips
- 1 liter milk
- 300 gm whipped cream

Preparation

1. In a bowl, combine all the ingredients and mix well.
2. Pour this mixture in the slow cooker and cook for 2.5 hours.

Serving

Serve this butterscotch chocolate hot and top it up with some more whipping cream if you want.

35) Banana Lemon pudding

Ingredients

- 3 eggs (yolks and whites beaten separately)
- 175 gm hung yogurt
- 1 teaspoons lemon zest
- 175 gm sugar
- 4 tablespoons flour
- 4 bananas (ripe ones), diced

Preparation

1. In a bowl. Mix the hung yogurt, egg whites, egg yolks, lemon zest and flour. Now add the bananas.
2. Grease the slow cooker with some butter, add the banana mixture and cook for 1.5 hour.
3. Let it sit for another 20 minutes.

Serving

Serve this pudding with some lemon slices on top.

Variation

You can also use orange zest instead of lemon.

36) Marshmallow chocolate fondue

Ingredients

- 400 gm semi-sweet chocolate (cubed)
- 250 gm marshmallows
- 100 ml double cream
- 100 gm graham crackers or nuts or waffles
- 1 tablespoon butter

Preparation

1. In a slow cooker, add some butter, chocolate, marshmallows and stir properly.
2. Cover the lid of the cooker and cook for 2.5 hours on slow heat. Keep stirring it gently until the mixture blends smooth without any lump formations.
3. Let it sit for about 15 minutes before you serve.

Serve

Serve the fondue a bit warm and serve it on low-heat setting along with graham crackers.

Variation

You can also use chocolate chips instead of whole chocolate.

37) Blueberry dumplings

Ingredients

- 400 gm fresh blueberries
- 2 tablespoon self-rising flour
- 200 gm biscuit mix
- 225 gm sour cream
- 2 teaspoons lemon zest
- 200 gm castor sugar

Preparation

1. Take a sauce pan, add sugar, flour, lemon zest and stir until smooth.
2. No add the blueberries and cook the mixture for about 12-15 minutes on medium heat until the

sugar is dissolved. Keep stirring the mixture so to make sure there are no lump formations.
3. Combine the biscuit mix, sugar, sour cream and make a soft dough.
4. Pour the blueberry mixture into a slow cooker and gently slide in 5-6 scoops of the dough.
5. Cook for about 3 hours.

Serving

You can serve the dumplings with some ice-cream or cherries on top.

Variation

You can also add a bit of lemon juice to add some tang to this dish.

38) Chocolate and peppermint pretzels

Ingredients

- 400gm pretzel nuggets
- 600 gm chocolate flavored candy (chopped)
- 300 gm semi-sweet chocolate (cubed)
- 300 gm peppermint candies
- 1/4th teaspoon peppermint essence

Preparation

1. Combine pretzel nuggets, chocolate candy, chocolate and mix well . Transfer this mixture to a slow cooker and cover with a lid.
2. Cook it on slow flame for 2 hours. Now add the peppermint candies and peppermint essence gently and give it a stir.

3. Take some pretzel mixture with the help of a spoon and place a scoop one by one on a parchment paper. Refrigerate them for 60 minutes. You can store these pretzels in an airtight container.

39) Crockpot Orange Cinnamon pudding

Ingredients

- 6 bread slices (cut into cubes)
- 100 gm raisins
- 400 gm reduced or thickened milk
- 4 eggs (beaten)
- 2 tablespoons butter (melted)
- 200 gm castor sugar
- ½ teaspoon cinnamon powder
- 1 teaspoon vanilla essence
- 175 ml orange juice

Preparation

1. In a bowl, combine milk, whisked eggs, melted butter, cinnamon, orange juice, sugar, vanilla essence and stir properly.

2. Grease the cake mould using some butter. Pour the orange mixture into the mould and place the mould on a metal rack.
3. Take some water in a slow cooker, place the metal stand inside it and cook the pudding for about 2.5 hours.

Serving

Drizzle some honey on top of this dessert.

Variation

You can replace the cinnamon powder with some orange zest.

40) Slow cooked apples with peanut butter

Ingredients

- 5 apples (sliced and peeled)
- 100 gm raisins
- 2 tablespoons self-rising flour
- 100 gm castor sugar
- 125 ml orange juice
- 1 teaspoon orange zest
- 125 ml water
- 2 tablespoons peanut butter
- 50 roasted peanuts (chopped)
- ¼ th teaspoon salt

Preparation

1. In a bowl, combine the raisins, flour, sugar, juice, orange zest and juice, water, peanut butter and blend well.
2. Transfer the mixture in a slow cooker and over with a lid.
3. Cook apples on slow heat for about 8 to 9 hours until the apples are tenderized.

<u>Serving</u>

Serve it with some whipped cream on top.

<u>Variation</u>

You can use almonds butter if you are not a bug peanut butter fan.

41) Banana Foster

Ingredients

- 4 bananas (rip, peeled and cubed)
- 100 gm brown sugar
- 50 ml coconut milk
- ½ teaspoon cardamom powder
- 150 gm chopped pineapple pieces
- 50 ml rum (dark)
- 2 scoops of vanilla ice-cream
- 2.5 tablespoons butter

Preparation

1. The first step is to grease the Crockpot with some cooking spray. Now combine sugar, milk,

butter, rum and cook these ingredients on slow heat for a good 60 minutes.

2. Later, add cardamom powder, pineapple and banana to this thick mixture and keep stirring continuously to coat them. Cover the lid of the slow cooker and cooker this mixture for another 15-17 minutes.

Serving

Serve the dish hot and top it up two scoops of vanilla ice-cream.

Variation

You can replace the pineapple with another tropical fruit like strawberry.

42) Tiramisu Pudding

Ingredients

- 50 ml water
- 75 gm brown sugar
- 400 ml milk
- 2 eggs (beaten)
- 1 tablespoon strong coffee
- 650 gm bread (cubed)
- 2 tablespoons Kahlua liquor
- 75 gm mascarpone cheese
- 2 ½ teaspoons cocoa powder (unsweetened)
- 3/4th teaspoon vanilla essence

Preparation

1. For the coffee mixture, combine water, sugar, coffee, cocoa powder and boil it for about 60 seconds. Switch off the flame, stir in the Kahlua liqueur.
2. In a bowl, take some milk, eggs and whisk them. Now add the coffee mixture to it.
3. Lay the bread pieces on a cake mould and transfer the mould onto a metal stand.
4. Take some 250 ml hot water in a Crockpot, place the metal stand in it and cook this pudding for about 2 hours on slow flame.
5. Mix mascarpone cheese with vanilla essence and whisk until smooth. Spread this mixture on the bread pudding.

Serving

Top it up with some heavy milk cream and serve in a large bowl.

Variation

You can skip the cocoa powder and use a little more coffee.

43) Coconut and Tapioca pudding

Ingredients

- 100 gm pineapple (diced)
- 450 ml coconut milk
- 1 egg
- 100 gm desiccated coconut
- 150 gm brown sugar
- 100 gm tapioca (cubed)

Preparation

1. IN a slow cooker, mix the tapioca, sugar, coconut milk and blend well. Now turn the heat on and cook it for 2 hours on slow heat until the tapioca turns translucent.

2. IN a bowl, take the eggs and whisk it using a beater, now add about 100 ml tapioca mixture to the eggs and stir well. Whisk again.
3. Pour it in the remaining tapioca mixture that is cooked in the Crockpot. Cook fro another 25 minutes on slow heat.

Serving

You can garnish this pudding with mango slices on top.

Variation

You can also use castor sugar instead of brown sugar.

44) Vanilla flavored pudding with Brandy

Ingredients

- 800 gm cubed bread
- 150 gm plums (chopped)
- 75 ml brandy
- 100 gm castor sugar
- 250 ml reduced milk
- 1 teaspoon vanilla essence
- 1/4th teaspoon salt
- 3 eggs (beaten)

Preparation

1. Marinate the plums in some brandy in a bowl. Leave this mixture for about an hour so the plums are completely soaked in the brandy.

2. Combine the brandy and plum liquid with milk, sugar, vanilla, salt, eggs and whisk for a minute.
3. Lay the bread cubes in a cake mould, pour the mixture on top of it and place the mould on a metal trivet.
4. Take some hot water in a Crockpot, place the trivet in the middle of the cooker and let the pudding cook for 4 hours.

Serving

Serve this pudding slightly warm.

Variation

You can use berries instead of plums.

45) Dark Apple Cake

Ingredients

- 300 gm self-rising flour
- 100 gm brown sugar
- 1 sliced apple
- 1 teaspoon baking soda
- 1 teaspoon cinnamon powder
- 1/4th teaspoon nutmeg powder
- 200 ml apples sauce
- 75 ml butter milk
- 50 gm butter (melted)
- 1 eggs (beaten)
- ½ teaspoon baking powder
- 1 teaspoon vanilla essence

Preparation

1. Combine all the dry ingredients in a bowl except the apples. Now in another bowl combine all the wet ingredients like eggs, vanilla essence, egg, butter, apple sauce and blend well.
2. Combine the dry and the wet mixture and whisk it using a beater.
3. Pour this mixture in a baking mould, transfer the mold on a metal trivet and place the apple slices on top of the mixture.
4. Take 250 ml water in a slow cooker, place the metal stand inside it and cook for 2.5 hours on medium heat.

Serving

Serve this cake alongside your morning cup of tea.

Variation

You can skip the apples and just use apple sauce.

46) Gooey Chocolate brownie cake

Ingredients

- 125 gm butter (melted)
- 300 gm castor sugar
- 125 gm cocoa powder
- 3 ½ tablespoons self-rising flour
- 1 teaspoon vanilla essence
- 100 gm chocolate chips
- 1/4th teaspoon salt
- 3 eggs (beaten)

Preparation

1. Combine all the dry ingredients in a bowl and mix well. In another bowl combine all the wet ingredients including chocolate chips and mix well.

2. Transfer the mixture on a cake mold and place the mold on a metal trivet.
3. In a slow cooker, take some water and place the metal trivet inside it. Cook for 3 hours on slow heat. The cake needs to be gooey from inside.

Serving

Always best served with a scoop of vanilla ice-cream

Variation

Use chocolate cubes instead of chocolate chips.

47) Cherry sauce to go with Angel Cake

Ingredients

- 450 gm fresh cherries (seeds removed)
- 100 ml apple juice
- 75 gm brown sugar
- 3 tablespoons amaretto
- 1 ½ tablespoons tapioca
- 500 gm angel cake (sliced)

Preparations

1. In a slow cooker, combine the cherries, sugar, amaretto, apple juice, tapioca and cook for 5 hours on slow heat. Let it stand for half an hour.
2. Now pout the cherry sauce on to the angel cake slices.

48) Slow Cooker Carrot cake

Ingredients

- 200 gm sugar
- 2 eggs (beaten)
- 300 gm self-rising flour
- 75 ml vegetable oil
- 50 ml water
- 1 teaspoon baking powder
- 3/4th teaspoon baking soda
- 1 teaspoon cinnamon powder
- 200 gm carrot (peeled and grated)
- 1 teaspoon vanilla essence

Preparation

1. In a bowl combine all the dry ingredients including grated carrot and mix well. In another bowl, mix together all the wet ingredients. Now combine the dry and the wet ingredients and stir again.
2. Pour the mixture in a baking mould and place the mold on a metal rack.
3. Take some hot water in the slow cooker, place the metal rack inside it and cook for 3 hours on slow flame.

Serving

Serve the cake with a dollop of whipped cream or honey on top.

Variation

Use the exact recipe.

49) Pumpkin Pie dip

Ingredients

- 400 gm pumpkin pie mix
- 125 gm cream cheese
- 50 ml sour cream
- A few chopped almond or walnuts

Preparation

1. Combine all the ingredients together in a bowl and mix well. Transfer this mixture to a baking mold and then onto a metal trivet.
2. Take some hot water in a slow cooker, place the metal trivet inside it and cook this pie dip for 1.5 hour.

Serving

You can serve assorted fruit slices or pretzels to go with this dip.

50) Slow cooked pear with apples

Ingredients

- 300 gm ripe apples (roughly chopped)
- 300 gm ripe pears (roughly chopped)
- 150 gm brown sugar
- 1/4th teaspoon salt
- ½ teaspoon cinnamon powder

Preparation

1. Grind the fruits in grinder until it forms a smooth paste.
2. Transfer the paste to a slow cooker, add sugar, salt, cinnamon powder and cook for about 3.5 hours without the lid on slow heat. You can

store this dip in an air-tight container and refrigerate it for about 20-22 days.

Serving

You can serve this dip with some nuts on top.

Variation

Use the same recipe.

From the Publishers:

We hope that you enjoyed some of Betty's favorite and most delicious dessert crockpot recipes that she has been making over the years in her very own kitchen for her family to feast on.

If 1 or some of these recipes are not suitable for specific individuals due to allergies, or health reasons then please understand that Betty is only trying to provide you with her best recipes that she can possibly provide.

Please feel free to give us an email at bettycrockpotrecipes@gmail.com rather than venting your dislike for any one of her recipes on the review pages of her books. We will gladly assist you in any way that we can.

Betty works hard to provide the best and most delicious recipes and does so with a great attitude and outlook on life.

We would like to keep the happy spirit flowing throughout, and are dedicated to promoting overall health and wellness for everyone!

Look out for more recipe books from Betty and if you found some of these recipes to be enjoyable please feel free to leave your kind words by way of reviews.

Thank you very much and enjoy!

Hey check this out!

Hey everyone I am Dexter, I am an Author and Publisher of many books in a wide variety of topics spanning from fiction to non - fiction.

I am helping Betty out by getting her books Published and spreading the word of her wonderful recipes to the general public.

I have got a couple of SPAM FREE newsletters that may be of interest to you.

Real World Nutrition Newsletter

This is a FREE newsletter pertaining to all of the wonderful things that go on in the health and nutrition world, Dexter's style! Check it out.

Dexter's SPAM FREE eBook deals of the month

This is another completely SPAM FREE newsletter that I have dedicated only to providing my subscribers information on new releases of mine and other Authors I deal with like Betty, and letting them in on sweet deals and drastic discounts, and even the occasionally FREE eBook giveaway!

I have many subscribers who love the fact that I have this separate newsletter that I have dedicated to letting them know about what is new and upcoming before it even gets out to the general public.

Check it out, it is 100% SPAM FREE!

You can email me at **dextersebooks77@gmail.com** for more details.

Check through my books, drop a comment, give me a like on my page over to the right if you want! I believe that I will keep all of Betty's recipe books over on my Authors page as well so you can check those out also.

I look forward to chatting with you soon!

Carpe Diem

Dexter

Disclaimer:

The information provided in this book is designed to provide helpful information on the subjects discussed. This book is not meant to be used, nor should it be used, to diagnose or treat any medical condition. For diagnosis or treatment of any medical problem, consult your own physician. The publisher and author are not responsible for any specific health or allergy needs that may require medical supervision and are not liable for any damages or negative consequences from any treatment, action, application or preparation, to any person reading or following the information in this book. References are provided for informational purposes only and do not constitute endorsement of any websites or other sources. Readers should be aware that the websites listed in this book may change. All rights reserved. No part of this book may be reproduced or transmitted in any form or by any means, electronic or mechanical, including photocopying, recording or by any information storage and retrieval system, without written permission from the author, except for the inclusion of brief quotations in a review.

Printed in Great Britain
by Amazon.co.uk, Ltd.,
Marston Gate.